Fret Not

A Comprehensive Guide To Taming Your Anxiety

Tiwayi Mushambi

Introduction

You've probably heard a version of the following statements:

"Don't worry about it."

"It's perfectly normal to be anxious about this kinda thing."

This seems to imply that there are things that are okay to worry about, and things you should just let go. If that's so, then who is the arbiter of what's worth stressing yourself over? In most cases, we thrust that authority upon ourselves. After all, who better to know which danger is most imminent to you?

This "danger", whatever it may be, is subjective to the individual in distress. For example, a teenager about to ask someone out for the first time might feel as though the world could end if they are unsuccessful. As adults, we now cringe when we think back to those memories, but the anxiety we felt (and sometimes still feel) at the prospect of rejection was justified in the moment.

A lot of negative emotions, like anger, feel justified in the moment. You feel justified to be angry when someone cuts you off on the freeway, just like you'd feel justified to worry about money after losing your job. Much like anger, anxiety can be validated by present circumstances, and both of them linger and grow until they are dealt with.

Let's say we chalk up the teen's anxiety to raging hormones and immaturity. Surely now, as an adult, you understand the gravity of *real* issues, right? Unfortunately, no matter how logical your reasons for worrying may be, it is still just as pointless.

When anxiety is persistent, excessive, or disproportionate to the circumstances, it becomes a disorder. The goal of anxiety management is to prevent the development of anxiety disorders and the negative effects anxiety has on your physical health, behavior and relationships.

Therefore, it is important to find healthy ways to manage anxiety, such as developing coping strategies, seeking professional help, practicing relaxation techniques, and engaging in self-care activities. You can't think your way out of a problem if your mind is consumed by the problem. That is why it is important to relax and assess situations objectively instead of going into a panic.

People often confuse anxiety management with quitting worry cold turkey. There is no immediate and permanent off switch for anxiety. Whether you're as stoic as a cyborg or a bundle of nerves, situations will always arise that will make us anxious. What's important is to face those anxious thoughts head on, challenge their validity and re-frame our thought patterns and actions, which is where Cognitive Behavioral Therapy (CBT) comes in.

CBT helps because it not only affects thoughts and feelings, but actions as well. Negative thoughts cause people to have negative emotions, which lead to destructive behaviors. When we are anxious, we engage in certain behaviors such as avoidance, procrastination, projection, and distraction. These behaviors cost us closure, time, perspective and productivity respectively.

CBT focuses on identifying unhealthy thought processes and correcting one's thoughts and beliefs, to stop them from escalating to feelings of anxiety or an unhealthy behavior in response to that.

CBT is an evidence-based practice and has been shown to be particularly effective in treating certain types of anxiety disorders. Research supports its effectiveness in treating anxiety disorders such as:

✓ Generalized anxiety disorder

✓ Panic disorder

✓ Phobias like Agoraphobia (Fear of places and situations that might cause panic, helplessness or embarrassment.)

✓ Social anxiety disorder

CBT is also used to treat other disorders where anxiety is a common symptom, including obsessive-compulsive disorder (OCD) and post-traumatic stress disorder (PTSD).

It goes without saying that this book is by no means a substitute for inter-personal therapy. However, it is a good start for those seeking to understand their anxiety and revisit the discussions therein at their discretion.

So, fret not. Enjoy your reading.

Chapter 1. Common Anxiety Triggers

After being inundated with a global pandemic, job losses, wars, inflation and murder hornets, I think it's safe to say that there is no shortage of things that induce anxiety in today's world.

Despite the prevalence of anxiety and trigger warnings, many people are still unaware of what really triggers anxiety. You may think that the events themselves are the triggers, but the real triggers are what affect how you react to negative situations.

We'll go through the most common ones and how you can manage your anxiety with each trigger.

1. Stress

Imagine a length of steel rod bearing a load of 1500 kilograms on one end. If you swing a sledgehammer hard enough, the steel will bend. Your blow may have provided the force required to bend the metal, but you're not the cause. That's how stress works. It stretches us beyond the point where we bounce back, until one of life's crushing blows comes along.

Stress is one of the significant contributors to anxiety. Whether it is related to work, school, or family, high levels of stress can lead to anxiety symptoms, such as insomnia, jitteriness, restlessness, and nervousness. While some stress is inevitable, it is essential to ensure that it does not overwhelm you.

Exercise:

One way to manage stress is to exercise. When life throws something at you that you can't control, throw yourself into something you can. Physical activity is not only beneficial for your body, but also an excellent stress reliever. Engaging in regular exercise helps release endorphins, our feel-good hormones, which promote a positive mood.

It can be as simple as taking brisk walks, jogging, yoga, or any physical activity you enjoy. Aim for at least 30 minutes of exercise daily, and you will be amazed at the positive impact it can have on alleviating stress.

Meditation:

Mindfulness and meditation are also powerful techniques that allow you to connect with the present moment and ease stress. By focusing on your breath and observing your thoughts without judgment, you can break free from stress-inducing worries. Even a few minutes of mindfulness or meditation each day can help calm your mind, reduce anxiety, and increase overall well-being.

Take good care of your health:

Adopting a healthy lifestyle is crucial for managing stress effectively. Ensure you get enough sleep, as lack of rest can exacerbate stress levels. Make time for healthy, well-balanced meals to nourish your body and boost your energy levels.

Avoid excessive caffeine, nicotine, and alcohol, as they can intensify feelings of stress. Taking care of your physical health promotes mental resilience and equips you to handle stress more effectively.

Find solace in nature:

Spending time in nature has a profound impact on reducing stress. Whether it's a stroll in the park, a hike in the mountains, or simply sitting in a garden, immersing yourself in natural surroundings can help calm your mind and invigorate your senses.

Research has shown that spending time in nature reduces cortisol levels, the hormone associated with stress, and promotes a sense of relaxation.

You can also combine going out in nature with other hobbies like painting landscapes or photography.

Foster Supportive Relationships:

Building and maintaining strong relationships is vital for stress management. Reach out to your loved ones, whether it's family, friends, or support groups, and share your thoughts and feelings. Talking through your stressors with someone you trust can provide emotional support and perspective.

Additionally, engaging in activities that foster positive social connections, such as joining clubs or volunteering, can also help alleviate stress and provide a sense of purpose.

Whatever tickles your fancy:

Various relaxation techniques, such as deep breathing exercises, progressive muscle relaxation, or listening to calming music, can effectively reduce stress levels. These techniques promote a state of relaxation, lower heart rate, and decrease muscle tension. Experiment with different techniques and incorporate them into your daily routine to discover what works best for you.

By implementing these practical strategies into your daily routine, you can actively combat stress, improve your overall well-being, and enhance your ability to handle life's challenges. Remember, self-care is essential, and taking time for yourself is not selfish but necessary for a happier and more fulfilling life.

2. Trauma

Unlike stress, the amount of emotional baggage that trauma brings comes as a flood instead of a trickle. Traumatic events such as assault, abuse, accidents, or loss of loved ones can leave you feeling vulnerable and anxious. People who have experienced trauma are more likely to develop anxiety disorders like Post Traumatic Stress Disorder (PTSD).

While it may seem challenging to overcome this type of anxiety, employing practical strategies can help you regain control of your life and move towards healing. We can't choose our trauma, but we can explore some effective ways to address trauma-induced anxiety.

Therapy:

When dealing with trauma-induced anxiety, it is crucial to seek support from qualified mental health professionals. Therapists, psychologists, or counselors experienced in trauma-focused therapy can provide the necessary guidance and support to help individuals navigate their emotions and develop coping mechanisms.

Therapy techniques such as Cognitive Behavioral Therapy (CBT) and Eye Movement Desensitization and Reprocessing (EMDR) have proven effective in treating trauma-related anxiety.

Relationships:

Building a strong support network is crucial when dealing with trauma-induced anxiety. Surround yourself with understanding and empathetic individuals who can provide emotional support. Connecting with support groups or seeking community resources can offer a safe space to share experiences, exchange coping strategies, and receive validation, thus reducing feelings of isolation.

Keep Busy:

Engaging in activities that bring you joy, practicing relaxation techniques, and prioritizing self-care routines can help reduce anxiety levels. This may include regular exercise, working on your business, maintaining a balanced diet, and participating in hobbies or activities that promote relaxation and fulfillment.

Silence the voices:

Trauma often leads to recurring negative thoughts and beliefs, like blaming yourself for being the victim. It is important to challenge and reframe these thought patterns. Identify negative self-talk and replace it with positive and realistic affirmations. This process may take time, but regularly practicing self-compassion and nurturing a positive mindset can gradually shift thought patterns and reduce anxiety.

Dealing with trauma-induced anxiety is a challenging journey, but there are practical ways to manage and overcome it. You've seen how seeking professional help, practicing mindfulness, establishing a support network, engaging in self-care, challenging negative thought patterns, and setting realistic goals are all strategies that can contribute to healing and a brighter future. Remember, healing is a process, and progress takes time – be kind to yourself along the way.

3. Health Scares

Although we are aware that our days are numbered, we seldom keep an eye on the countdown. However, a doctor's prognosis is sometimes accompanied by the dreaded number we rarely think about, giving form to the proverbial deadline. This concern can lead to significant distress and impact our overall well-being.

However, it is vital to understand that while a medical diagnosis provides critical information about our health, it does not solely determine our fate. With the advent of modern medicine, we now see more remissions, recoveries and an increase in longevity. For example, in the '80s, it was considered a death sentence to be HIV positive. But we now know that with treatment and lifestyle changes, one can continue living a full life for decades.

One of the most powerful weapons against health anxiety is knowledge. Educate yourself about your genetic predispositions. Medical conditions and treatments that concern you.

Also, learn about how you can provide your body with the nutrition it needs to fight or prevent disease. There is no shortage of 'superfoods' in the average supermarket, and they are usually cheaper than junk food.

Consult with healthcare professionals or other trusted sources to gather accurate information. Understanding the science behind medical conditions, risk factors, and advancements in medical treatments can alleviate irrational fears and provide a broader perspective.

Play your part:

While genetics may play a role in certain conditions, lifestyle factors often have a significant impact on overall health. Emphasize the aspects within your control, such as adopting a balanced diet, engaging in regular physical activity, managing stress, getting adequate sleep, and quitting harmful habits like smoking or excessive alcohol consumption. Small yet consistent changes can significantly reduce the risk and severity of many illnesses.

Dealing with genetic anxiety can be overwhelming, and nobody should have to face it alone. Reach out to support networks such as friends, family, or support groups. Connecting with individuals who have experienced or are going through similar challenges can provide valuable emotional support and help alleviate feelings of isolation. Additionally, professional therapy or counseling sessions with mental health experts can equip you with coping techniques and strategies tailored to your specific concerns.

Cultivating a positive mindset is crucial when combating health anxiety. Instead of focusing solely on worst-case scenarios, remind yourself of the realm of possibilities beyond your genetics. Engage in activities that bring you joy, practice mindfulness and stress reduction techniques, and surround yourself with positivity. Adopting an optimistic outlook and celebrating small victories can help shift the focus from anxiety to empowerment.

Health anxiety can pose significant challenges, but it's essential to remember that we can actively participate in our own well-being. By educating ourselves, making positive lifestyle choices, seeking support, and utilizing available resources such as genetic testing and counseling, we can effectively manage and overcome medical anxiety. Embrace the power of taking control and look forward to a healthier future where your well-being is governed by your choices rather than solely by your genetic makeup.

4. Social situations

Social anxiety is a type of anxiety that is triggered by social situations such as public speaking, meeting new people, or going to public events like parties. While everyone experiences social anxiety at some point, those with Social Anxiety Disorder (SAD) experience intense feelings of fear and avoidance in social situations.

One of the core aspects of social anxiety is the presence of negative thoughts and self-doubt. You don't need to mentally undress everyone around you in order to make yourself feel better. Instead, engage in a process called cognitive restructuring, which involves identifying and challenging these negative thoughts.

Replace them with more realistic and positive ones to help reframe your perspective on social situations. For example, you may have social anxiety because you believe yourself to be boring or uninteresting. Instead of focusing on what you think makes you boring, try to draw out what you find interesting in others and provide feedback. Ask questions like, "what are you most excited for this week?"

Exposure therapy is an effective technique for gradually facing feared social situations. Start by listing situations that trigger your social anxiety and rank them in order of difficulty. Begin with the least challenging situation and expose yourself to it repeatedly until the anxiety lessens. Gradually progress to more challenging scenarios over time.

Using relaxation techniques like deep breathing, progressive muscle relaxation, and mindfulness meditation can help reduce anxiety levels in social situations. Regularly practicing these techniques will equip you with coping mechanisms to manage anxiety as it arises.

Working on improving your social skills can significantly enhance your confidence. Engage in role-playing exercises with a trusted friend or family member to practice social interactions. This can include initiating conversations, maintaining eye contact, and active listening. With time and practice, these skills will become more natural and boost your confidence in social situations.

Taking care of your physical and mental well-being is essential for managing social anxiety. Incorporate self-care activities such as regular exercise, a nutritious diet, sufficient sleep, and hobbies that help you unwind. Regular exercise and good nutrition improve your appearance and confidence, and hobbies supply you with engaging stories to tell and people to meet. Prioritizing self-care enhances overall resilience and equips you to face social situations more effectively.

5. Environmental factors

Environmental factors like bright lights, loud noises, and closed spaces can also trigger anxiety. These stimuli can be overwhelming for some people, like those with Claustrophobia, Phonophobia or PTSD, and can lead to anxiety symptoms.

While it is not always possible to avoid anxiety triggers, learning to manage stress and seeking professional help can help alleviate symptoms and improve quality of life.

Understanding Claustrophobia:

Claustrophobia is commonly defined as a fear of confined or enclosed spaces. To overcome claustrophobia, it is essential to gradually expose oneself to the fear-triggering situations in a controlled manner.

This process involves gradually increasing exposure to confined spaces while practicing relaxation techniques such as deep breathing, progressive muscle relaxation, or mindfulness. With time, you'll find yourself stepping into an elevator without giving it a second thought.

Seeking professional help from a therapist or counselor who specializes in anxiety disorders can provide additional guidance and support throughout the recovery process.

Managing Phonophobia:

Phonophobia is the fear or aversion to specific sounds or loud noises. Similar to claustrophobia, exposure therapy plays a crucial role in overcoming this anxiety disorder. Gradually exposing oneself to the fear-inducing sounds in a controlled environment can help desensitize the individual over time.

Additionally, cognitive-behavioral therapy (CBT) techniques, such as thought challenging and reframing, can assist in reshaping negative thoughts and emotions associated with certain sounds. The goal is to build resilience and develop coping mechanisms that allow for a more balanced and comfortable response to triggers.

Coping with PTSD:

PTSD is a complex anxiety disorder that can develop after experiencing or witnessing a traumatic event. The symptoms can include flashbacks, nightmares, hyper arousal, and avoidance behaviors. Seeking professional help is crucial for managing PTSD effectively.

Treatment options may include trauma-focused therapy, cognitive processing therapy (CPT), eye movement desensitization and reprocessing (EMDR), or medication in more severe cases. Integrative approaches like mindfulness, relaxation techniques, and support groups can also contribute to the recovery process.

Another way to cope with PTSD is to practice gratitude. After all, you survived a traumatic event and get to live another day. Focus on relationships with the people you thought you would never see again. Show them how much you appreciate them and the chance you have to be with them again.

Conclusion

In conclusion, while we can't itemize every cause of anxiety, these cover the majority of what we all face at some point or another. You can't always control what happens to you, but you can control what disturbs your inner peace. To paraphrase the words of Bruce Lee, be more like water, which conforms to whatever container it finds itself in, but when focused, can even cut through metal.

Chapter 2. Anxiety Behaviors and Defense Mechanisms

All living things have three options whenever they face danger: fight, flight or freeze. These three Fs materialize differently with each individual, resulting in the various defense mechanisms and behaviors we exhibit when we are anxious about something.

In order to cope with anxiety, people often develop defense mechanisms or behaviors to protect themselves from the discomfort and distress associated with this mental health condition. We will go through a comprehensive overview of anxiety behaviors and defense mechanisms, shedding light on how they manifest and how individuals can regain control over their lives.

Types of Anxiety Behaviors:

Avoidance:

One common behavior stemming from anxiety is avoidance. Individuals may avoid situations, people, or places that trigger their anxiety, leading to missed opportunities and reduced quality of life.

Causes of Avoidance Anxiety Behavior:

1. Past Traumatic Experiences: Anxiety can develop as a result of traumatic experiences such as accidents, abuse, or witnessing a distressing event. Individuals may avoid situations reminiscent of those traumatic events to prevent re-triggering intense anxiety.

2. Learned Behaviors: People may develop avoidance anxiety behaviors by observing avoidance in others, particularly during their formative years. This learned behavior engrains the belief that avoiding certain situations is an effective coping mechanism.

3. Fear of the Unknown: Uncertainty about unknown situations or fear of negative outcomes can contribute to avoidance anxiety. The apprehension of potential risks or negative consequences leads individuals to avoid facing their fears.

Effects of Avoidance Anxiety Behavior:

1. Limited Life Experiences: Avoidance anxiety behavior significantly restricts an individual's ability to engage in numerous activities. By fearing anxiety-inducing situations or objects, they may avoid social gatherings, public speaking, never leaving their comfort zones. This limited engagement can hinder personal and professional growth.

2. Interpersonal Challenges: Avoidance behavior often affects relationships as individuals may avoid socializing or attending important events. This can strain personal connections, causing frustration, misunderstandings, and isolation.

3. Reinforcing Anxiety: Avoiding anxiety-triggering situations or objects often leads to short-term relief. However, by avoiding these experiences, individuals unintentionally perpetuate anxiety in the long run as they never fully confront their fears. A mountain of what-ifs sustains anxiety, making it increasingly difficult to overcome.

Procrastination:

Anxiety can often lead to procrastination as individuals feel overwhelmed and struggle to cope with their anxious thoughts and feelings, leading to a delay in completing tasks.

Causes of Procrastination Anxiety Behavior:

1. Fear of failure: One of the primary causes behind procrastination anxiety behavior is the fear of failure. People who struggle with this often believe that if they don't try, they won't have to face the possibility

of not succeeding. This fear stems from a deep desire to preserve one's self-esteem and avoid the pain of disappointment.

2. Perfectionism: Perfectionists tend to set incredibly high standards for themselves, leading to a constant fear of not meeting those expectations. This fear can paralyze individuals, causing them to procrastinate as a way to avoid potential criticism or feelings of inadequacy.

3. Overwhelming or ambiguous tasks: When faced with overwhelming or ambiguous tasks, individuals may experience anxiety about where to start, how to proceed, and whether they will be able to complete the task successfully. As a result, they may put off starting the task, hoping to find a better time or obtain more clarity.

Effects of Procrastination Anxiety Behavior:

1. Increased stress and anxiety: Procrastination anxiety creates a cycle of increased stress and anxiety. As deadlines loom closer, individuals experience heightened stress levels, leading to a sense of overwhelm and panic. This, in turn, further exacerbates their anxiety and perpetuates the cycle of procrastination.

2. Decreased productivity and performance: Procrastination significantly hampers productivity and performance. When tasks are continuously delayed, individuals find themselves rushing to complete them at the last moment, resulting in subpar outcomes. This further reinforces negative self-beliefs and self-doubt.

3. Damage to mental well-being: The constant struggle with procrastination anxiety can take a toll on an individual's mental health. Feelings of guilt, inadequacy, and disappointment can lead to increased levels of depression, lower self-esteem, and a decreased sense of self-worth.

Excessive worrying:

Chronic worrying is a prevalent behavior among individuals with anxiety. It involves persistent and intrusive thoughts about potential negative outcomes, even when there is no immediate threat.

Causes of Excessive Worrying:

Excessive worrying can have multiple underlying causes, involving a combination of genetic, environmental, and psychological factors. Some individuals may have a genetic predisposition to anxiety disorders, making them more prone to excessive worrying.

Additionally, environmental stressors, such as traumatic experiences, unhealthy relationships, or major life changes, can contribute to the development of excessive worrying behavior. It is important to keep in mind that each individual's experience may be unique, and the causes can vary greatly from person to person.

Symptoms of Excessive Worrying:

Individuals struggling with excessive worrying may experience a range of emotional, cognitive, and physical symptoms. Emotionally, they may feel intense fear, unease, or a constant sense of impending doom. Cognitively, their thoughts may be dominated by excessive negativity, catastrophic thinking, and an inability to control their worry.

Physical symptoms like increased heart rate, trembling, sweating, shortness of breath, and a tense or restless feeling within the body are also common manifestations of excessive worrying. These symptoms often interfere with daily functioning, leading to significant distress and impairment in various areas of life.

Impact on Daily Life:

Excessive worrying and anxiety behavior can have a profound impact on personal relationships, occupational performance, and overall well-being. Individuals may encounter difficulties in maintaining healthy relationships due to constant apprehension and fear that may lead to misunderstandings or excessive dependence on others.

Moreover, the accompanying physical symptoms may make it challenging to concentrate and perform well in academic or professional settings. Chronic worrying can also disrupt sleep patterns, triggering fatigue, irritability, and reduced productivity. Overall, excessive worrying can create a vicious cycle of negative thoughts and behavior, ultimately compromising one's quality of life.

Common Defense Mechanisms:

Denial:

Denial allows individuals to refuse or minimize anxiety-inducing situations or emotions. They may convince themselves that everything is fine, avoiding necessary acknowledgment and addressing of underlying issues.

The Function of Denial:

Denial serves several functions when employed as a defense mechanism for anxiety. It acts as a psychological shield, protecting individuals from confronting overwhelming emotions or circumstances that can exacerbate anxiety.

By refusing to acknowledge or accept these stressors, individuals create a mental barrier that shields them from immediate distress, allowing them a temporary respite. Denial can also provide a sense of control by maintaining the illusion of stability, preventing anxiety from infiltrating one's daily life.

Consequences of Denial:

While denial may offer immediate relief from anxiety, it can also lead to significant consequences in the long run. By evading reality, individuals fail to address the root causes of their anxiety, postponing essential personal growth and problem-solving.

Denial can perpetuate a cycle of avoidance, further exacerbating anxiety and limiting opportunities for personal development. In addition, repressing anxiety through denial can contribute to intensified emotional distress, potentially leading to psychosomatic symptoms, strained relationships, and a decreased ability to effectively manage anxiety in the future.

Repression:

Repression is an unconscious defense mechanism where distressing thoughts, memories, or emotions are pushed out of conscious awareness, shielding individuals from facing their anxiety.

Understanding Repression:

Repression, first introduced by Sigmund Freud, refers to the unconscious exclusion of ideas, memories, and desires from conscious awareness. It acts as a psychological shield, preventing threatening or anxiety-provoking experiences from reaching conscious perception. By pushing these thoughts into the subconscious, repression attempts to alleviate the immediate distress associated with anxiety.

Role of Repression in Anxiety:

Anxiety stems from the fear of unknown outcomes, failures, or potential harm. When faced with anxiety-inducing situations, individuals may employ repression as a defense mechanism to avoid confronting these distressing emotions head-on. By burying the source of anxiety in the unconscious, individuals may temporarily find relief from the immediate discomfort. However, this relief is often temporary, and repression can lead to other psychological consequences.

Mechanisms of Repression:

Repression functions at an unconscious level, creating an internal divide between conscious and unconscious content. Unwanted thoughts and memories are suppressed into the unconscious, making them less accessible to conscious awareness. This process often involves the deployment of various cognitive strategies such as selective attention, rationalization, and denial. Over time, these mechanisms solidify, creating an effective barrier against the threatening thoughts that underlie anxiety.

Long-Term Consequences of Repression:

While repression may provide temporary relief from anxiety, its long-term consequences can be detrimental to mental well-being. By repressing anxiety-inducing thoughts and emotions, individuals may inadvertently heighten their psychological distress.

Repressed thoughts can resurface as unconscious symbols, disguised in dreams, slips of the tongue, or in various psychosomatic symptoms. Furthermore, unresolved anxiety may manifest into chronic conditions such as generalized anxiety disorder or even contribute to the development of more severe mental disorders.

Projection:

Projection involves attributing one's anxiety-inducing thoughts or emotions to another person or object, shifting blame or responsibility away from oneself.

The Function of Projection as an Anxiety Defense Mechanism:

Projection serves several psychological functions in protecting individuals from anxiety. Firstly, it allows individuals to distance themselves from their own unwanted feelings by attributing them to others. By projecting feelings of anger, aggression, or jealousy onto someone else, individuals create psychological distance and alleviate their own discomfort. This defense mechanism enables them to preserve a positive self-image and avoid acknowledging unconsciously suppressed aspects of their personality.

Secondly, projection can also provide relief from anxiety by diminishing feelings of guilt or shame. When individuals project their own perceived flaws or inadequacies onto others, they divert attention away from their own self-perceived shortcomings. This alleviates the anxiety associated with maintaining a coherent and positive sense of self.

Manifestations and Consequences:

Projection can be observed in various forms. For instance, individuals may project their anxieties onto specific groups or individuals, labeling them as a threat to deflect attention from their own insecurities. Additionally, projection can manifest as the exaggeration or distortion of another person's traits, causing them to be seen in a negative light. Such distortions provide a false sense of superiority and protection against one's own inner turmoil.

While projection may provide temporary relief, it can have negative consequences. Misattributed emotions or thoughts can strain relationships, causing misunderstandings and conflicts. Moreover, projecting one's own unresolved issues onto others can impede personal growth and prevent individuals from facing their anxieties directly.

Rationalization:

Rationalization is the process of creating logical or plausible explanations to justify or minimize anxious thoughts or behaviors, allowing individuals to maintain a sense of control and avoid confronting the underlying anxiety.

Function of Rationalization in Anxiety Management:

Rationalization serves as a psychological strategy to protect an individual's self-esteem and reduce anxiety by creating psychological distance from the real reasons behind their thoughts or actions. It acts as a shield against uncomfortable truths, allowing individuals to convince themselves that their actions or beliefs are acceptable and logical, even when they might not be.

Benefits of Rationalization:

1. Ego preservation: Rationalization helps individuals preserve their sense of self-worth and protect their ego. By constructing intellectually plausible explanations, individuals can maintain a positive self-image and prevent feelings of guilt or shame that might arise from acknowledging their true motivations or behaviors.

2. Minimizing discomfort: Rationalization provides a psychological buffer from the discomfort that arises from cognitive dissonance — the tension caused by conflicting beliefs or values. It allows individuals to reduce the anxiety associated with contradictory thoughts or actions by providing an alternative explanation that supports their existing beliefs or desires.

3. Emotional regulation: Rationalization helps individuals regulate their emotions by offering a seemingly logical justification for their behaviors. It can provide a sense of relief, allowing individuals to rationalize away anxiety-inducing thoughts or actions and maintain a sense of control and stability in their lives.

Drawbacks and Limitations:

While rationalization can serve as a short-term coping mechanism, it is important to acknowledge its limitations and potential drawbacks:

1. Self-deception: Rationalization can lead to self-deception, where individuals convince themselves of their desired reality, blurring the line between truth and falsehood. This evasion of reality can hinder personal growth and problem-solving, as it prevents individuals from addressing genuine concerns or taking responsibility for their actions.

2. Hindering personal development: Relying on rationalization as a defense mechanism may prevent individuals from exploring and addressing the root causes of their anxieties. By avoiding self-reflection, they may miss opportunities for personal growth and fail to adapt to challenging situations.

3. Strained relationships: Rationalization can strain relationships with others, as it may involve making excuses or denying responsibility for one's actions. This defensive behavior can erode trust, hinder effective communication, and contribute to conflict or misunderstanding.

Healthy Coping Strategies:

a. Cognitive-Behavioral Therapy (CBT): CBT focuses on identifying and challenging negative thought patterns and developing healthier coping mechanisms to manage anxiety symptoms effectively.

b. Mindfulness and Meditation: Practicing mindfulness and meditation can help individuals gain awareness of their anxious thoughts and emotions, allowing them to observe and detach from them without judgment.

c. Physical Activity: Engaging in regular exercise promotes the release of endorphins, which can improve mood, reduce anxiety, and help individuals regain a sense of control.

d. Seeking Support: Talking to a trusted friend, family member or seeking professional help from therapists or counselors can provide individuals with valuable support and guidance in managing anxiety.

Conclusion:

Understanding anxiety behaviors and defense mechanisms is crucial in developing effective strategies to manage and overcome anxiety-related challenges. While anxiety can be debilitating, individuals can regain control by recognizing their behaviors, learning healthier coping mechanisms, and seeking appropriate support. By taking proactive steps, individuals can navigate anxiety with resilience and lead fulfilling and empowered lives.

Disclaimer: The information provided in this article is for educational purposes only and should not be substituted for professional advice. Please consult a qualified mental health professional for personalized assistance with anxiety-related concerns.

Chapter 3. Cognitive-Behavioral Therapy (CBT)

Cognitive-behavioral therapy (CBT) is a type of treatment that focuses on identifying and changing negative thoughts and behaviors that contribute to anxiety. Here are a few examples of how CBT can be used to help deal with anxiety:

1. Recognizing and challenging negative thoughts

When you feel anxious, your mind may be filled with negative thoughts about the situation or yourself. CBT involves identifying these thoughts and examining them to see if they are realistic or not.

For example, if you're anxious about a job interview, you might be thinking, "I'm going to fail this interview, and I'll never get hired." This thought can make you feel more anxious and discouraged. In this case, a CBT therapist might encourage you to challenge this thought and replace it with a more positive one like, "I've prepared well for this interview, and I'll do my best."

1. Using relaxation techniques

Relaxation techniques like deep breathing, progressive muscle relaxation, and visualization can help you calm down when you feel anxious. CBT therapists can teach you these techniques and help you practice them so they become a habit when you're faced with anxiety-provoking situations.

1. Learning coping strategies

CBT can equip you with various coping skills such as problem-solving, time-management, assertiveness communication and goal setting. This can help you to manage anxiety by breaking down the issue into smaller goals, prioritizing tasks, developing communication skills and setting yourself up to achieve success with better chances.

1. Exposure Therapy or "Facing your fears"

Gradually exposing yourself to your fears or anxiety triggers. This might mean gradually approaching a feared situation (e.g., public speaking) or deliberately enduring the physical sensations of anxiety (e.g., purposeful twitching). This can help you realize that you can survive and eventually cope with anxiety and fears.

Remember, CBT is an evidence-based approach to anxiety treatment that works for many people. So, it's essential to consult a qualified therapist to guide you through therapy, customize a treatment plan, and apply specific techniques to your situation and monitor your progress.

Common CBT Techniques for Anxiety

Once problematic thought and behavior patterns have been identified, CBT therapy will focus on teaching skills to help people replace these patterns with other, more helpful patterns. CBT therapy tends to be very solution-focused, with the therapist working closely with the client towards specific goals.1

Here are some common CBT techniques used to treat anxiety symptoms:

Anxiety Psychoeducation

For any disorder, CBT will provide a level of psychoeducation to inform the client about their particular anxiety disorder, how symptoms form, how they are maintained, and the proposed course of action. This phase of treatment could only take a few minutes or a few sessions, depending on the complexity of the situation and someone's understanding of their anxiety.

Pattern Tracking

The goal of CBT treatment is to reduce symptoms and improve functioning by changing thought and behavior patterns. To help achieve that goal, early treatment is often focused on helping clients recognize these patterns and find ways to stop them before they become problematic.

Common CBT pattern tracking assignments include logs where clients are asked to track their:

- Thoughts they have throughout the day, especially during times they experience stress or anxiety (for example, any "what-if" thoughts that increase anxiety)
- Emotions they experience and the intensity of these emotions (e.g., slight nervousness vs complete panic)
- Behaviors and responses when anxious, and any consequences or rewards these behaviors lead to (e.g., noticing avoidance relieves short term anxiety but increases long term anxiety)
- External or internal circumstances that cause specific thoughts, feelings, and responses (e.g., anxiety triggered by certain social situations or when thinking about the unknown)

Thought Stopping

Once awareness of patterns is developed, CBT therapists may begin to teach specific skills to interrupt and replace some of the client's patterns. Many CBT skills focus on helping clients interrupt unhelpful thought patterns, but some also focus on helping clients interrupt unhelpful patterns of behavior. Once interrupted, the client learns ways to replace these thoughts and behaviors with patterns that are more helpful.

Thought stopping is a skill that involves using a verbal or visual mental command when experiencing unhelpful thoughts that interrupts them. This may be the word "Stop" or "No," or imagining an image of a stop sign when a person begins replaying an embarrassing moment or worrying about something that hasn't happened yet.[9]

Reframing Thoughts

Reframing is a skill that involves interrupting an unhelpful thought and then trying to rethink it in a more helpful way. For example, a person could reframe an anxious thought about an upcoming doctor's appointment by thinking about the ways it could benefit their health.

Reframing can help people adjust their thoughts in ways that reduce anxiety and lead to more effective responses. Reframing works by helping to introduce more rational thinking patterns during times when a person's thinking has become overly emotional.

Reframing thoughts is especially beneficial to those who struggle with their self-esteem. A person who undergoes this type of technique is asked to challenge a certain view they have of themselves to check if it's real or not.

Challenging Thoughts

Challenging thoughts involves testing the accuracy of a thought through rational processes like listing evidence for whether the thought is true or untrue, or considering other viable explanations. Challenging anxious thoughts can reduce anxiety and also reduce irrational and impulsive decisions during times of stress or worry.

For instance, listing the evidence for and against a certain belief or assumption is a common CBT method of challenging irrational thoughts. This skill can help people recognize when their thoughts might be distorted because of their anxiety, instead of automatically believing they are true.6,9

Exposure Tasks

Because anxious people tend to avoid situations that make them anxious, exposure tasks are often recommended to limit avoidance, reduce anxiety, and build confidence. Exposure tasks involve gradually facing feared situations and building up to more intensely feared and avoided situations.

For example, a person afraid of public speaking might start by practicing a speech in front of one or two friends and progress to speaking to a small group at work. CBT therapists also teach clients relaxation skills (like deep breathing or muscle relaxation) to prepare for these exposures. Exposures work by helping people gain confidence in their ability to face their fears, while also developing the skills to better manage their anxiety.10

Problem Solving

Problem solving involves clients being encouraged to think through the options and evaluate the potential short- and long-term consequences of each option. Because many anxiety-driven behaviors are focused only on finding short-term relief, these skills are needed to help them make better decisions.

For instance, canceling plans might be tempting for someone with social anxiety because it would mean avoiding an uncomfortable situation but it can lead to isolation, depression, and even more social anxiety in the long run. Using a problem solving approach could identify these consequences ahead of time, helping a person avoid making a poor choice in the moment.

Behavioral Activation

Anxiety tends to make people less active socially and behaviorally. People may think that doing less and avoiding their problems lowers anxiety, but it actually increases symptoms. Therefore, therapists will work to get the person going places, doing things, and engaging with others to lessen the impact of anxiety.

Relaxation Skills

Exposure and behavioral activation activities will induce higher levels of anxiety in the short-term. Learning and using relaxation skills can help to cushion the impact of anxiety and decrease symptoms sooner and more efficiently.

Journaling

Asking the client to journal their thoughts, feelings, and behaviors is a frequently used CBT tool. The process can help the client understand themselves and their experience, but it can also help the therapist better understand the person and their point-of-view. Using anxiety journaling prompts can be a great way to start tracking your symptoms and understand what may be the underlying triggers associated with your anxiety symptoms.

What are the different types of CBT?

The type of treatment you receive depends on the issues being addressed. Different types of cognitive therapy can include:

Mindfulness-Based Cognitive Therapy (MBCT)

This form of cognitive behavioral therapy combines cognitive behavioral therapy with meditation and helps cultivate a worthless, present-oriented attitude called mindfulness.

MBCT can effectively help you manage: anxiety disorder, depression and Bipolar disorder.

Dialectical Behavior Therapy (DBT)

Dialectical behavior therapy (DBT) is another type of evidence-based cognitive therapy that uses strategies such as problem solving and acceptance seeking. DBT is very effective in treating strong emotions and serious mental illnesses. Those who benefit from DBT tend to see things in black and white. You see situations one way or the other.

You may not be able to see a middle ground or find a grey area. DBT may be able to help if you lack coping skills and find yourself transitioning from one crisis to another. Dialectical behavior therapy can also help you learn the skills you need to deal with it more effectively. DBT is known to help people struggling with: Borderline Personality Disorder; Bipolar disorder; substance abuse; ADHD; Food disorders and Post Traumatic Stress Disorder (PTSD).

Acceptance and Commitment Therapy (ACT)

This behavioral CBT technique relies heavily on positive reinforcement and counter-conditioning. ACT's purpose is to change the way you respond to your inner experiences.

Inner experiences include:

- Emotions
- Thoughts
- pulses
- Physical feelings

Acceptance and Commitment Therapy teaches you how to stop denying, avoiding, and struggling with your inner emotions. You learn to recognize the deepest feelings. During speech therapy, you may begin to realize that your feelings may be an appropriate response to certain situations. Once you understand this mindset, you can begin to accept the difficulties and problems you encounter. This acceptance allows you to make the behavioral changes needed to improve your life.

ACT can help you learn to manage:

- severe depression
- social anxiety disorder
- work stress
- psychosis
- Obsessive Compulsive Disorder (OCD)

- Test anxiety
- chronic pain
- addiction and chemical dependency

Rational Emotional Behavioral Therapy (REBT)

REBT is an active therapy approach that helps you identify irrational beliefs such as self-destructive feelings and thoughts. You will learn to actively challenge irrational thoughts and eventually recognize and change your thought patterns. Ultimately, REBT teaches you to replace negative thoughts with healthier, more productive beliefs. REBT is one of the types of CBT that has been shown to be effective in treating people with: severe depression; explosive or extreme anger and Bad eating habits.

Therapeutic Techniques of CBT

The type(s) of cognitive therapy treatment(s) you receive will depend on the areas of life you wish to address in talk therapy. There are a number of types of CBT treatment techniques that mental health providers will employ. Some of the most common treatment techniques are:

Cognitive Restructuring/Remodeling

By taking a close look at your negative thought patterns, you can begin to transform them into more productive and positive thought patterns. This CBT technique can be helpful if you tend to overgeneralize, overemphasize relatively insignificant things, or constantly assume that the worst outcome is inevitable.

Exposure Therapy

This is an excellent CBT technique for treating phobias and overcoming fears. Exposure therapy helps you cope with the things you find most difficult in life. By gradually exposing you to the thing you fear, the mystique and anxiety towards it loses its potency. Ultimately, exposure therapy can help you gain confidence and feel less vulnerable in certain situations.

Role Playing Game

If you can reproduce scenarios that normally cause stress or anxiety in your life, you can learn to change your behavior. Role play has been shown to be successful in developing healthy problem-solving skills, gaining confidence and assertiveness, improving communication skills, and defining and enhancing social skills.

Meditation

During a meditation practice, areas of concentration include inner thoughts, breathing sensations, sounds and specific parts of the body. When your mind starts wandering, you learn to bring your attention back to the things you were focusing on. Some believe that the practice of Tai Chi and yoga helps to focus and develop awareness of the breath.

Diaries

In CBT, various writing activities are often used. Listing negative thoughts and positive affirmations can both be a helpful way to grow between therapy sessions. You can also follow new thought patterns and behaviors you are learning as you watch them happen. This can be an effective way to track your journey's progress, which can be very motivating.

Progressive Muscle Relaxation

To apply progressive muscle relaxation, you learn to stretch a specific muscle group or body part for 5 to 7 seconds and then rest for up to 30 seconds. This technique can be helpful in learning the difference between relaxation and tension.

Sure, I could walk you through an anxiety therapy session, but it's important to note that therapy sessions can vary depending on the individual needs of the client and the therapeutic approach used by the therapist. What's important is that you learn the skills and techniques listed above for use when you are outside the safe space of your therapist's office.

Chapter 4. Negative Thought Patterns

Have you ever looked at yourself in one of those carnival funhouse mirrors? Part of the fun is seeing a form that you know is not your own. Squiggly, skinny or brawny doppelgangers of your image. It is a distortion of the image you possess in your mind. Much like those mirrors, we sometimes unknowingly view our situations through 'cognitive distortions'.

Cognitive distortions are biased or exaggerated ways of thinking that can lead to inaccurate perceptions or negative emotions. They are often automatic and subconscious, and can contribute to anxiety, depression, and other mental health issues. Here are some examples of common cognitive distortions:

1. **All-or-nothing thinking:**

This is when you see things as black-and-white, with no middle ground. For instance, you might think "I got one bad grade, so I'm a complete failure."

Recognizing and overcoming this cognitive distortion is essential for promoting balanced thinking and emotional well-being. In this article, we will explore effective strategies to overcome the all-or-nothing cognitive distortion and cultivate a more nuanced perspective. Understanding All-or-Nothing Thinking: All-or-nothing thinking, also known as black-and-white or dichotomous thinking, involves viewing situations, people, or outcomes in rigid, polarized terms.

This distortion often manifests as absolute statements, such as "I must be perfect" or "If I fail once, I'm a complete failure." It leaves no room for flexibility or recognizing the complexity of life. Strategies for Overcoming All-or-Nothing Thinking: **1.** Identify and Challenge

Extremist Thoughts: Begin by becoming aware of the all-or-nothing statements in your thoughts.

When faced with a situation, pay attention to any extreme judgments you make. Question the evidence and consider alternative possibilities. Is it realistic to see things only in absolute terms? Practice finding the grey areas and moderate viewpoints that lie between the extremes.

Embrace Imperfection:

Perfectionism often fuels all-or-nothing thinking. Recognize that striving for perfection is both unrealistic and unnecessary. Accept that making mistakes and experiencing setbacks are natural parts of life. Focus on progress rather than striving for unattainable ideals. Embracing imperfections allows for growth and reduces the pressure of black-and-white expectations.

Seek Grey Area:

Challenge yourself to think in shades of grey. Instead of labelling things as either good or bad, try to find the middle ground. Understand that most situations aren't solely positive or negative but instead possess a combination of both. This mindset cultivates open-mindedness and enables a more balanced and realistic perspective.

Practice Cognitive Restructuring:

Cognitive restructuring involves consciously replacing negative and extreme thoughts with more accurate and rational ones. Once you identify an all-or-nothing thought, evaluate the evidence supporting it. Look for alternative interpretations and consider the shades of gray. Replace absolutist statements with statements that reflect a more nuanced understanding of the situation.

Develop Self-Compassion:

All-or-nothing thinking often stems from harsh self-judgment. Practice self-compassion by being kind and understanding towards yourself. Treat yourself as you would a close friend who is facing challenges. Be patient with your progress, celebrate small successes, and learn from failures without falling into absolutes.

Conclusion: Overcoming the all-or-nothing cognitive distortion is essential for promoting a balanced and healthy mindset. By identifying and challenging extreme thoughts, embracing imperfections, seeking middle ground, practicing cognitive restructuring, and cultivating self-compassion, you can break free from the confines of all-or-nothing thinking.

With time and effort, you can develop a more nuanced perspective and enjoy a more flexible and fulfilling life. Remember, life is rarely black and white; it is the shades of grey that make it beautiful.

1. Overgeneralization:

This is when you make broad conclusions based on one or a few examples. For example, if you fail a job interview, you might think "I'll never get hired anywhere."

Overgeneralization occurs when we draw far-reaching conclusions based on isolated incidents or instances. For example, if someone receives criticism for a particular presentation at work, they might generalize it by believing they are bad at presentations overall, leading to self-doubt and avoidance of future opportunities. This distortion can lead to a skewed perception of reality, hindering personal growth and causing unnecessary emotional distress.

Recognize the Overgeneralization:

The first step in overcoming overgeneralization is recognizing when this cognitive distortion is at play. Self-awareness is key. Pay attention to your thoughts and emotions in various situations. Notice if you tend to make sweeping negative assumptions or believe that one setback predicts future failures.

Challenge Your Thoughts:

Once you've identified overgeneralization, challenge the thoughts that reinforce it. Examine the evidence supporting your belief, and consider alternative explanations or counterexamples. Ask yourself if there might be other interpretations or if your belief is based on a single incident rather than a pattern of experiences. This process helps to create a more rational and balanced perspective.

Seek Diverse Perspectives:

Often, our overgeneralizations are fueled by our own biases or limited exposure to different viewpoints. Engage in conversations with others who have different experiences, beliefs, or expertise. This can broaden your understanding and challenge the rigid thinking behind overgeneralizations. By gaining new perspectives, you can reduce the tendency to make sweeping conclusions based on limited information.

Build Resilience with Positive Experiences: Overgeneralization tends to focus on negative or unfavorable experiences, ignoring positive outcomes or successful moments. Counteract this bias by actively seeking out and acknowledging positive experiences. Practice gratitude by keeping a journal of daily achievements, no matter how small. This helps to rewire your brain to recognize a wider range of experiences and break the tendency towards overgeneralizations.

Challenge Core Beliefs:

Overgeneralizations often stem from deeply ingrained core beliefs about ourselves, others, or the world. Take time to reflect on these beliefs and critically evaluate their accuracy. Ask yourself if your core beliefs are based on concrete evidence or if they are distorted by past experiences, societal influences, or personal insecurities. Challenging and reframing these core beliefs can be transformative in overcoming overgeneralization.

Practice Mindfulness:

Mindfulness techniques, such as meditation or deep breathing exercises, can help you become more present and aware of the present moment. By practicing mindfulness, you can detach from automatic negative thoughts associated with overgeneralization and focus on the reality of the situation. This empowers you to respond to events more effectively, reducing the tendency to jump to unwarranted conclusions.

Seek Professional Help:

In some cases, cognitive distortions like overgeneralization may persist despite your best efforts. Seeking the help of a mental health professional, such as a therapist or counselor, can provide additional support and guidance. They can help you identify underlying causes, provide effective strategies tailored to your situation, and facilitate lasting change.

Conclusion:

Overcoming overgeneralization cognitive distortion requires persistence, self-reflection, and a willingness to challenge our own thoughts and beliefs. By implementing the strategies mentioned above and seeking professional help when needed, we can develop a healthier and more accurate perspective on ourselves, others, and the world around us. Remember, breaking free from the bounds of overgeneralization opens the door to personal growth, resilience, and emotional well-being.

1. Jumping to conclusions:

This is when you assume you know what someone else is thinking or what will happen without any evidence. For example, if a friend doesn't call you back, you might think "They must be mad at me."

It involves filling in informational gaps with unrealistic or negative interpretations, leading to erroneous conclusions. These premature judgments can hinder our ability to be objective, empathetic, and open-minded.

Recognize the Signs:

To overcome this cognitive distortion, it is crucial to first recognize its signs and become aware of the impact it has on our thoughts and behaviors. Some common signs include making assumptions without verifying, overgeneralizing, mind-reading or assuming others' intentions, and catastrophizing situations based on incomplete information.

Challenge Your Assumptions:

One effective strategy for overcoming jumping to conclusions is to challenge the assumptions and beliefs that fuel these hasty judgments. Whenever you catch yourself making quick judgments or forming opinions without solid evidence, pause and ask yourself: "What evidence do I have to support this conclusion?" By questioning the basis for your belief, you can encourage a more balanced and rational perspective.

Seek Additional Information:

Often, jumping to conclusions stems from gaps in knowledge or misunderstandings. To combat this, make a conscious effort to seek additional information before drawing conclusions. Engage in active listening, ask open-ended questions, and approach situations with a mindset of curiosity. This approach not only enhances your knowledge but also helps you form a more accurate understanding of the situation.

Practice Mindfulness:

Mindfulness is a powerful tool in overcoming cognitive distortions. By practicing mindfulness, you learn to observe your thoughts without judgment and become more aware of the present moment. This awareness enables you to recognize when you are jumping to conclusions and provides an opportunity to redirect your thinking towards a more rational and evidence-based approach.

Consider Alternative Explanations:

Another valuable technique is to consider alternative explanations or perspectives. Challenge yourself to evaluate different viewpoints, even if they contradict your initial assumptions. By doing so, you broaden your understanding and develop a more comprehensive picture of a situation, reducing the likelihood of jumping to conclusions.

Develop Empathy:

Empathy plays a crucial role in overcoming cognitive distortions. Cultivate empathy by putting yourself in others' shoes and considering their circumstances and motivations. Recognize that people's behaviors may stem from various factors beyond your initial assumptions. Developing empathy fosters understanding, compassion, and a more accurate interpretation of others' actions.

Conclusion:

Overcoming the jumping to conclusions cognitive distortion is a key step towards developing rational thinking and improving our overall well-being. By making a conscious effort to challenge our assumptions, seek additional information, practice mindfulness, consider alternative explanations, and develop empathy, we can break the cycle of hasty judgments and make more informed decisions. Remember, it takes time and practice, but with dedication, we can embrace a more rational and balanced approach to understanding the world around us.

1. Catastrophizing:

This is when you imagine the worst-case scenarios and assume they will definitely happen. For example, if you lose your job, you might think "I'll never find another one and I'll end up homeless."

Catastrophizing can lead to increased anxiety, stress, and a distorted view of reality. Thankfully, there are effective strategies that can help us overcome this cognitive distortion and cultivate a more balanced perspective. In this article, we will explore some practical techniques to overcome catastrophizing and foster a healthier mindset.

Recognize and Challenge Negative Thoughts:

The first step in overcoming catastrophizing is to become aware of the negative thoughts as they arise. Take a moment to pause and acknowledge that the thoughts may be distorted and exaggerated. Challenge these thoughts by asking yourself questions like, "Is there evidence to support this catastrophic outcome?" or "What are some alternative, more realistic perspectives on this situation?"

Practice Mindfulness:

Engaging in mindfulness exercises can help you distance yourself from catastrophizing thoughts. By observing your thoughts without judgment, you can create space to evaluate their validity objectively. Techniques such as meditation, deep breathing exercises, or simply being fully present in the moment can all help in reducing the tendency to catastrophize.

Reframe Negative Statements:

Instead of dwelling on worst-case scenarios, consciously reframe negative statements into more balanced ones. Replace catastrophic thoughts with more realistic, constructive, and optimistic statements. For example, instead of thinking "This awful situation will ruin everything," reframe it as "Challenges are an opportunity for growth, and I can find solutions to overcome them."

Gather Evidence:

To counter catastrophizing, gather objective evidence that contradicts your catastrophic thoughts. Look for examples from your past experiences that demonstrate your ability to handle difficult situations. Reflecting on these instances will provide you with a more balanced perspective and boost your confidence in dealing with challenging circumstances.

Seek Perspective from Others:

When we catastrophize, our thoughts tend to be stuck in a self-centered loop. Seeking perspective from others can provide valuable insights and shift our focus beyond our own fears. Discuss your concerns with trusted friends, family, or a mental health professional. They can help challenge your catastrophic thoughts and provide alternative viewpoints that offer a more realistic assessment of the situation.

Set Realistic Goals and Focus on Solutions:

Breaking down overwhelming tasks into smaller, manageable goals can prevent catastrophizing. Create a step-by-step action plan that allows you to focus on practical solutions rather than fixating on worst-case scenarios. By taking proactive steps towards resolving issues, you'll regain a sense of control and minimize catastrophizing tendencies.

Conclusion:

Overcoming catastrophizing cognitive distortion is a journey that requires conscious effort and practice. By recognizing and challenging negative thoughts, practicing mindfulness, reframing statements, gathering evidence, seeking perspective from others, and focusing on solutions, you can cultivate a more balanced perception of reality. Embracing these techniques will help you reduce anxiety, manage stress, and approach life's challenges with greater resilience and emotional well-being. Remember, it's through transforming your thinking patterns that you can find freedom from the grip of catastrophizing and embrace a more positive outlook on life.

1. **Emotional reasoning**:

This is when you believe your feelings are facts. For example, if you feel anxious in a social situation, you might think "I must be in danger here."

With awareness and practice, one can overcome emotional reasoning and cultivate a more balanced perspective. In this article, we will explore some effective strategies to help overcome this cognitive distortion and regain emotional clarity.

Recognize Emotional Reasoning:

The first step towards overcoming emotional reasoning is to recognize its presence in our thoughts and actions. Emotional reasoning often manifests as statements such as "I feel this way, so it must be true" or "If I'm upset about it, it must be terrible." By acknowledging these tendencies, we can begin to separate emotions from facts and challenge our automatic thinking patterns.

Challenge Your Thoughts:

Once you identify emotional reasoning, it's essential to challenge and question the underlying thoughts or beliefs. Ask yourself if there is any evidence to support your emotional conclusion. Consider alternative explanations and different perspectives. Engage in logical reasoning and critical thinking to evaluate the validity of your thoughts rather than relying solely on emotions.

Seek Evidence and Objective Information:

To counter the grip of emotional reasoning, actively seek out objective information and evidence. This could involve doing research, seeking expert advice, or consulting reliable sources. Look for facts, statistics, or logical reasoning that can help you form a more balanced view of the situation. By relying on concrete evidence, you can avoid getting entangled in emotional biases.

Embrace Mindfulness and Self-Awareness:

Developing mindfulness and self-awareness techniques can be immensely valuable in overcoming emotional reasoning. Mindfulness practices, such as meditation or deep breathing, help individuals observe their thoughts and emotions without judgment. By cultivating a non-reactive and non-judgmental mindset, you can become more aware of how emotions influence your thoughts and actions.

Challenge Core Beliefs:

Often, emotional reasoning is rooted in deeply ingrained core beliefs that may be irrational or unhelpful. Identify these core beliefs and critically examine their validity. Ask yourself if these beliefs are based on evidence or if they stem from emotional reactions. By challenging and reframing these core beliefs, you pave the way for healthier and more rational thinking patterns.

Seek Support:

Breaking free from emotional reasoning can be challenging, especially if you've been caught in its grip for a long time. Seeking support from friends, family, or even a therapist can be immensely helpful. Talk to someone you trust about your thoughts and emotions, and seek their objective perspective. A supportive network can provide guidance, feedback, and a different viewpoint that can break emotional reasoning patterns.

Conclusion:

Overcoming emotional reasoning cognitive distortion requires conscious effort and practice. By recognizing emotional reasoning, challenging thoughts, seeking objective information, embracing mindfulness, challenging core beliefs, and seeking support, you can gradually break free from its grasp. Remember, fostering emotional clarity not only enhances decision-making but also promotes overall well-being and healthier relationships. With determination and the right strategies, you can overcome emotional reasoning and regain control over your thoughts and actions.

1. **Personalization:**

This is when you take things too personally and assume they are all about you. For example, if someone doesn't return your smile, you might think "They must not like me."

Personalization cognitive distortion is often fueled by negative self-talk and an internal dialogue that reinforces feelings of guilt and blame. Begin to question the validity of these thoughts by asking yourself, "Am I truly responsible for this? Are there other factors at play?" Replace negative self-talk with self-compassion and understand that not everything can be attributed to personal fault.

Identify External Factors:

In overcoming personalization cognitive distortion, it's crucial to recognize external factors that contribute to various outcomes. Practice perspective-taking and consider alternative explanations for negative events. Understand that the actions, intentions, and circumstances of others can influence outcomes, and it's not always about your actions alone.

Seek Different Perspectives:

Engage in open conversations with trusted friends, family, or professionals who can provide alternative perspectives on the situations that trigger personalization cognitive distortion. They can offer insights that challenge your distorted thinking patterns and help you see the bigger picture. Seeking different viewpoints fosters a more realistic understanding of events and reduces the tendency to personalize everything.

Practice Mindfulness and Self-Reflection:

Cultivate mindfulness and self-reflection as essential tools in overcoming personalization cognitive distortion. Mindfulness allows you to observe your thoughts and emotions without judgment, promoting a more objective view of yourself and your experiences. Through self-reflection, identify any underlying patterns or triggers that contribute to your personalization tendencies.

Focus on Personal Growth and Realistic Expectations:

Shift your attention towards personal growth rather than dwelling on the past or blaming yourself excessively. Set realistic expectations for yourself and accept that mistakes are part of the learning process. Learning from failures and setbacks can contribute to personal growth and resilience, reducing the tendency to engage in personalization cognitive distortion.

Practice Self-Compassion:

Developing self-compassion is crucial in overcoming personalization cognitive distortion. Treat yourself with kindness, understanding, and forgiveness. Remind yourself that everyone makes mistakes and that nobody is perfect. Acknowledge your efforts and achievements, and remember that setbacks do not define your worth as a person.

Conclusion:

Overcoming personalization cognitive distortion is a journey that requires self-awareness, a willingness to challenge negative thinking patterns, and a commitment to mental and emotional well-being. By recognizing the distortion, challenging negative self-talk, considering external factors, seeking different perspectives, practicing mindfulness and self-reflection, focusing on personal growth, and cultivating self-compassion, you can gradually diminish the impact of personalization cognitive distortion and foster a healthier mindset. Remember, your worth extends far beyond any individual outcome or event, and a more balanced perception of reality can lead to greater emotional well-being.

Identifying these cognitive distortions and challenging them with more realistic and balanced thoughts can help improve your mental health and overall well-being.

Chapter 5. Stoicism

In a fast-paced and unpredictable world, anxiety has become an increasingly prevalent issue for many individuals. While modern medicine and therapy provide effective solutions, there is an age-old philosophy that offers a unique perspective on managing anxiety: Stoicism. Stoicism, developed in ancient Greece and practiced by notable philosophers like Epictetus and Marcus Aurelius, teaches us how to navigate life's challenges with clear-headedness, resilience, and an inner sense of tranquility. In this article, we will explore how the principles of Stoicism can provide a valuable framework for tackling anxiety and enhancing overall wellbeing.

Understanding Stoicism:

Stoicism is a practical philosophy that emphasizes the cultivation of virtues such as wisdom, self-control, and courage. Its core teachings revolve around the notion that while we cannot control external events, we can control our own thoughts, emotions, and actions. By adopting a stoic mindset, individuals can transform their perception of anxiety and develop effective strategies to manage it.

Acceptance of the Uncontrollable:

Anxiety often stems from a fear of the unknown or a desire to control outcomes beyond our grasp. Stoicism teaches us to focus on accepting the things we cannot change and directing our attention towards what is within our control. By shifting our mindset, we minimize the energy wasted on worrying about external factors and direct it towards meaningful actions and self-improvement.

The Power of Perspective:

Stoicism challenges us to reframe our perspective on anxious thoughts and situations. Instead of catastrophizing or dwelling on worst-case scenarios, Stoics encourage rational thinking and the practice of internal dialogue. By questioning our anxious thoughts, we can evaluate their validity and challenge their influence over our emotions. This cognitive dissection empowers individuals to uncover the irrationality of anxiety and replace it with logical reasoning and a heightened sense of clarity.

Embracing the Present Moment:

Anxiety often thrives on anticipation and regrets of the past. Stoicism invites us to focus on the present moment, cultivating mindfulness and gratitude. By shifting our attention to the here and now, we become more attuned to the beauty of everyday experiences and find solace in the simplicity of life. This practice of being present allows us to detach ourselves from anxiety's grip and fully engage with the joys and challenges of each passing moment.

Building Resilience:

Stoicism teaches us the value of resilience in the face of adversity. By cultivating inner strength and fortitude, we become better equipped to navigate life's uncertain terrain. Stoics believe that embracing discomfort and challenges is an essential part of personal and spiritual growth. Viewing anxiety as an opportunity for self-improvement, we develop increased mental resilience, emotional stability, and the ability to bounce back from setbacks with renewed vigor.

Conclusion:

Stoicism offers a unique and valuable approach to managing anxiety by providing actionable insights and practical tools. By harnessing the power of acceptance, perspective, present moment awareness, and resilience, individuals can conquer anxiety and cultivate a sense of inner peace and tranquility. Remember, Stoicism is not about suppressing emotions but embracing them in a rational and constructive manner. By integrating Stoic principles into daily life, we can navigate anxiety with newfound wisdom and joy while maximizing our overall wellbeing.

Chapter 6. Adopting a Positive Mindset

Here are some ways to adopt a positive mindset to combat anxiety:

1. **Practice gratitude:**

Focus on the things you are thankful for instead of worrying about the things you don't have or the situations that make you anxious. Write down things you are grateful for each day, even if they seem small.

While there is no one-size-fits-all solution to anxiety, practicing gratitude has proven to be a powerful tool in managing and even overcoming anxiety symptoms.

Starting a gratitude journal is an excellent way to cultivate a positive mindset and shift your focus away from anxious thoughts. Each day, take a few moments to write down three things you are grateful for. These could be simple things like a warm cup of tea, a supportive friend, or a beautiful sunrise. By recognizing and appreciating the positives in your life, you gradually train your mind to seek out the good, reducing anxiety-inducing thoughts.

Anxiety often stems from dwelling on the past or worrying about the future. Mindfulness, on the other hand, encourages us to focus on the present moment. By practicing mindfulness, you become more aware of your surroundings, thoughts, and emotions, allowing you to better manage anxiety triggers. Incorporating gratitude into mindfulness exercises can enhance the experience further. As you tune into the present moment, take a moment to express gratitude for the sensations, experiences, and lessons life has provided you.

Make a conscious effort to spend time with people who uplift you, inspire you, and encourage your personal growth. Expressing gratitude to your loved ones not only strengthens your relationships but also fosters a sense of belonging and support. Share your appreciation for them by affirming their presence in your life, letting them know they make a positive difference in your journey.

Self-reflection allows us to gain insight into our thoughts, actions, and emotions. It's an opportunity to observe our patterns and beliefs and make necessary changes. While self-reflection is an introspective practice, incorporating gratitude into this process can counter negative self-talk and promote self-acceptance. Expressing gratitude for your strengths, accomplishments, and resilience can boost self-esteem and alleviate anxiety caused by self-doubt.

Helping others not only brings joy and fulfillment but also enables us to gain a new perspective on our own lives. Engaging in acts of kindness through volunteering or charitable activities allows you to recognize the blessings in your life and appreciate the positive impact you can make. By practicing gratitude through giving, anxiety can be reduced as we shift our focus from our worries to the power of compassion and making a difference in the world.

2. Visualize success:

We're not talking about "manifesting" your best life. Have you ever noticed how when you're introduced to someone new, you start seeing them everywhere? It's not because that person has begun stalking you (hopefully). It's because they are now on your radar and you notice them more. Picture yourself succeeding in the things that make you anxious. This helps you train your brain to think positively and can create positive feelings.

Steps to Visualize Success:

Set Clear Goals: Begin by establishing specific and realistic goals that you aim to achieve. When you have a clear target in mind, it becomes easier to visualize success in reaching that goal.

Create a Mental Movie: Close your eyes, relax, and imagine yourself in a calm, quiet space. Now, visualize achieving your goal in vivid detail. Imagine the steps you take, the actions you perform, and the positive emotions you experience along the way. Engage all your senses and feel the joy, satisfaction, and confidence of achieving your desired outcome.

Embrace Emotions: It's crucial to feel the emotions associated with your success. Allow yourself to experience excitement, pride, and confidence during the visualization process. Connecting emotions to your mental images intensifies their impact and strengthens your belief in the possibility of success.

Consistency is Key: Incorporate visualization into your daily routine. Set aside a few minutes every day to visualize success, even during moments of anxiety or doubt. Consistency reinforces positive thinking patterns and increases the effectiveness of visualization.

Take Inspired Action: Visualizing success is important, but it must be followed by tangible actions. Identify the steps needed to achieve your goals and take consistent and inspired action towards them. Visualization provides motivation and clarity, but it is the combination of visualization and action that propels us towards success.

3. Practice self-care:

Make sure you're taking care of yourself by getting enough sleep, eating a balanced diet, and exercising regularly. Taking care of your physical health can help you feel more positive and less anxious.

Self-care practices not only nurture your emotional and physical well-being but also promote resilience, balance, and inner peace. This article aims to explore effective self-care strategies that can empower you on your journey to overcoming anxiety.

Prioritize Mind-Body Connection: Nurturing the mind-body connection is essential to combat anxiety. Engaging in activities that promote relaxation, such as yoga, meditation, deep breathing exercises, or engaging in hobbies and creative outlets can help reduce stress levels. Make time for these practices regularly, even if it's just for a few minutes each day. By consciously focusing on your breath and being present in the moment, you can cultivate a sense of calm and gain control over anxiety-inducing thoughts.

Exercise and Physical Activity: Regular physical activity is not only beneficial for your physical health but also plays a vital role in managing anxiety. Engaging in exercises like jogging, dancing, swimming, or yoga boosts endorphin levels, which are natural mood enhancers. Additionally, physical activity helps in regulating sleep patterns, reducing muscle tension, and improving overall cognitive function. Choose activities that you enjoy and make it a habit to incorporate movement into your daily routine.

Establish Healthy Boundaries: One crucial aspect of self-care involves setting clear boundaries to protect your mental health. Learn to say no to activities or people that drain your energy and cause undue stress. Prioritize your well-being by allocating time and space for self-reflection, relaxation, and rejuvenation. By respecting your boundaries, you create an environment conducive to healing and promoting emotional balance.

Nourish your Body with Healthy Habits: Maintaining a nutritious diet is a fundamental aspect of self-care and plays a pivotal role in managing anxiety. Avoid excessive caffeine and sugar intake, as they can exacerbate anxiety symptoms. Opt for whole foods, including fruits, vegetables, lean proteins, and whole grains. Adequate hydration is also essential for optimal brain function and emotional well-being. Treat your body with kindness and fuel it with wholesome foods that nurture your mind and soul.

Cultivate a Supportive Network: Building a strong support system is essential for managing anxiety and promoting self-care. Surround yourself with individuals who uplift and support you emotionally. Seek out people who understand your struggles and empower you on your path to recovery. Additionally, consider joining support groups or therapy sessions to connect with others experiencing similar challenges. Sharing your experiences and listening to others' journeys can provide a sense of validation and encouragement.

Practice Positive Self-Talk: The way we speak to ourselves greatly influences our emotional well-being. It is crucial to challenge negative, self-defeating thoughts and replace them with positive affirmations. Remind yourself of your strengths, capabilities, and resilience. Reframe negative thoughts into empowering ones, fostering self-belief and confidence. Developing a positive self-talk routine can gradually rewire your brain to focus on optimism and resilience.

4. Find support: Share your feelings with friends, family, or a counselor who can give you positive reinforcement. Being around positive people can also help foster a more positive outlook.

Remember, adopting a positive mindset takes time and practice, but with perseverance, you can improve your mental health and overcome anxiety.

Chapter 7. Becoming Insouciant

Insouciant (in-sue-sea-ant). Very few people know what the word means, and even fewer people experience it. Being insouciant refers to a state of being worry-free. That is, being unruffled, unconcerned or nonchalant. When was the last time you ever felt that way? Completely at peace without an issue in the back of your mind?

The lucky ones can probably point to their childhood insouciance, but some of us were just as plagued by anxiety back then as we are now. While it is difficult to be naturally insouciant, we can still accomplish this state of mind by following a practical mind map of all our anxiety and clearing the slate.

Here is a detailed practical mind map of how to think through personal problems:

1. Identify the problem: Start by identifying the problem you are facing and write it down. Did you lose your job, or get bad news from the doctor? What is the challenge you are currently facing? Give your problem a name and write it down.

2. Define the problem: Clearly define the problem and all its aspects. For example, unemployment means no guaranteed source of income, which means your rent, food and other bills are at risk of not getting paid on time, which means you might become homeless and hungry. Drill down to the core of why your current problem bothers you.

3. Gather information: Gather as much information as possible about the problem. This can include past experiences, expert opinions, and research. Continuing with our unemployment example, find out if you can appeal the decision, what other jobs are available and what skills and resources you have to make a living.

4. Identify possible solutions: List all the possible solutions and alternatives to the problem. Use the information you gathered to create possible alternatives for you to consider. When one door closes, other doors open. Sometimes we obsess so much over a door we barely got a foot in that we forget about other opportunities that are outside our comfort zone.

5. Evaluate each solution: Evaluate each solution and weigh up the pros and cons of each. Do a SWOT analysis (Strengths Weaknesses Opportunities and Threats) of each of the alternate paths you can take. You'll rarely find a sure thing, so just focus on the solution that gives you the best odds of success.

6. Consider the consequences: Consider the potential consequences of each solution – both positive and negative. What if you fail? What if you succeed? It's also at this stage that you consider the morality behind your solutions. Most people would lie, cheat and steal to get out of trouble, but is that what you want?

7. Make a decision: Based on the evaluation of each solution, make a decision on the best course of action. Having evaluated each solution and considered the consequences, choose a path and stick to it. The only thing that should change your course of action is new information.

8. Create a plan of action: Once a decision has been made, create a plan of action outlining the steps needed to implement the solution.

9. Take action: Take the necessary action to implement the chosen solution. Remember, procrastination only provides temporary relief but compounds anxiety in the long run. As one great shoe company once said, "Just do it."

10. Evaluate the outcome: Evaluate the outcome of the solution to determine if it has effectively solved the problem.

11. Learn from the experience: Take advantage of the benefits of hindsight. Learn from the experience and apply any lessons learned to future problem-solving situations.

12. Reflect: Reflect on the process and identify ways to improve future problem-solving skills.

This mind map is just a guide and can be adapted to suit individual needs. Remember, problem-solving is an ongoing process, and with practice, it becomes easier to tackle even the most complex personal problems.

Embracing a Carefree State of Mind

Understanding the Concept of Insouciance:

Before embarking on the journey to become insouciant, it is crucial to grasp the meaning and essence of this state of mind. Insouciance involves freeing oneself from excessive concern about things outside of one's control.

It does not imply dismissing responsibilities or becoming indifferent; rather, it suggests shifting one's focus towards the present moment, accepting what cannot be changed, and directing energy towards constructive actions.

Prioritizing and Letting Go of Control:

One of the key components of insouciance involves recognizing and accepting the limits of one's control. Identifying personal priorities and learning to let go of control over uncontrollable aspects of life can significantly contribute to a carefree mindset. Differentiating between situations that require active involvement and those beyond one's control will allow individuals to channel energy wisely, reducing unnecessary stress and cultivating insouciance.

Embracing Imperfection and Laughter:

Insouciance thrives on the acceptance of imperfections and the ability to laugh, even in the face of adversity. Embracing mistakes as opportunities for growth, lightening up through humor, and not taking oneself too seriously can help maintain a carefree attitude. Laughter releases tension, boosts mood, and reminds us not to sweat the small stuff, contributing to the development of insouciance.

Living in the Present Moment:

Insouciance thrives in the present moment. Practicing mindful living and focusing on the present can divert attention from future worries and regrets of the past. Engaging in activities that bring joy and fulfillment, such as hobbies, spending time with loved ones, or pursuing creative outlets, encourages immersion in the present while cultivating a carefree mindset.

While becoming truly insouciant might not be easily attainable, adopting a more carefree attitude can significantly enhance a person's overall well-being and quality of life.

Embracing strategies such as self-awareness, reframing perspectives, letting go of control, embracing imperfection, and living in the present moment can empower individuals to become more carefree and insouciant. By embarking on this journey, you can experience newfound serenity, resilience, and a profound sense of freedom in an ever-challenging world.

FINAL SUMMARY

Living an anxiety-free life is a goal that many individuals aspire to achieve. However, achieving a state of freedom from anxiety is not an easy task, as it requires a conscious effort, self-awareness, and a holistic approach to one's physical, mental, and emotional well-being. It necessitates understanding the nature of anxiety, identifying triggers, and developing strategies to manage and overcome anxious thoughts and feelings. Moreover, building a support system, practicing self-care, cultivating positive habits, and embracing a mindset of resilience are essential pillars to living a more serene and anxiety-free life.

First and foremost, a fundamental understanding of anxiety and its impact on our lives is crucial. Anxiety is a natural response to stress or threats that help our bodies and minds prepare for danger. However, prolonged and excessive anxiety can be debilitating, negatively affecting our mental and physical health, relationships, and overall quality of life. Recognizing the signs and symptoms of anxiety, such as constant worry, restlessness, irritability, and physical tension, is the first step toward managing and ultimately overcoming it.

Next, identifying triggers and addressing them is essential in living an anxiety-free life. Triggers can be specific situations, people, or thoughts that incite heightened anxiety levels. By identifying these triggers, we can work toward minimizing or avoiding them whenever possible. Additionally, it is crucial to challenge negative and irrational thinking patterns that fuel anxiety. Engaging in cognitive-behavioral therapy or seeking professional help can be invaluable in this journey. By reframing negative thoughts and replacing them with more positive and realistic ones, we can diminish anxiety's grip on our lives.

Moreover, building a support system is vital for a life free from anxiety. Surrounding ourselves with understanding and compassionate individuals provides us with a sense of belonging and security. Sharing our fears and concerns with loved ones or joining support groups can offer valuable perspectives, coping mechanisms, and reassurance. Support from others helps us feel seen, understood, and not alone in our struggles. Additionally, professional support, such as therapy or counseling, can equip us with techniques and tools to manage anxiety effectively.

Furthermore, prioritizing self-care is paramount in pursuing a life devoid of anxiety. Engaging in activities that promote relaxation, such as exercise, deep breathing exercises, meditation, or mindfulness, can significantly reduce anxiety levels. Regular physical activity has been shown to enhance mood, reduce stress, and strengthen mental well-being. Nourishing our bodies with nutritious and balanced meals, ensuring proper sleep, and engaging in activities that bring joy and fulfillment contribute to overall mental resilience and emotional well-being. It is essential to establish boundaries and make time for self-care rituals regularly.

In addition to self-care, cultivating positive habits and routines can significantly impact anxiety levels. Engaging in activities that promote positive thinking, such as gratitude journaling, focusing on accomplishments, and seeking silver linings in challenging situations, can help retrain our minds to focus on the positive aspects of life. Setting achievable goals and celebrating small victories can boost self-confidence and reduce anxiety about the future. Incorporating relaxation techniques, such as deep breathing or visualization exercises, into our daily routines can assist in managing anxiety in stressful situations.

Finally, adopting a mindset of resilience is paramount in living a life free from anxiety. Embracing the understanding that setbacks and challenges are a part of life and that we have the ability to adapt and overcome them is crucial. Cultivating self-compassion, learning from past experiences, and embracing a growth mindset can help us view anxiety as an opportunity for personal growth and transformation. Accepting that setbacks may occur, but they do not define us, allows us to move forward with resilience and determination.

Also by Tiwayi Mushambi

The First Victory - The Power of Self-Discipline
It's Not Easy, But It's Simple
Fret Not: A Comprehensive Guide To Taming Your Anxiety